RETRO KIDS
Patterns and Prints

What Baby Baby Boomers Wore

DOVER PUBLICATIONS, INC.
MINEOLA, NEW YORK

Copyright

Copyright © 2011 by Dover Publications, Inc.
Electronic images copyright © 2011 by Dover Publications, Inc.

Bibliographical Note

Retro Kids Patterns and Prints: What Baby Baby Boomers Wore is a new work, first published by Dover Publications, Inc. in 2011.

DOVER *Pictorial Archive* SERIES

This book belongs to the Dover Pictorial Archive Series. You may use the designs and illustrations for graphics and crafts applications, free and without special permission, provided that you include no more than ten in the same publication or project. (For permission for additional use, please write to Permisions Department, Dover Publications, Inc., 31 East 2ⁿᵈ Street, Mineola, N.Y. 11501.)

However, republication or reproduction of any illustration by any other graphic service, whether it be in a book or in any other design resource, is strictly prohibited.

International Standard Book Number
ISBN-13: 978-0-486-48535-5
ISBN-10: 0-486-48535-8

The accompanying CD-ROM contains both high- and low-resolution JPEG files of each individual image. Although some of the images have been cropped for graphic effect in the book, the entire image is offered on the CD-ROM. The "Images" folder on the CD contains two different folders. All of the high-resolution files have been placed in one folder, and the Internet-ready files are in another folder. Every image has a unique file name in the following format: xxx.JPG. The first 3 digits of the file name, before the period, correspond to the number printed under the image in the book. The last 3 letters of the file name "JPG," refer to the file format. So, 001.JPG would be the first file in the folder.

Also included on the CD-ROM is Dover Design Manager, a simple graphics editing program for Windows that will allow you to view, print, crop, and rotate the images.

For technical support, contact:
Telephone: 1 (617) 249-0245
Fax: 1 (617) 249-0245
Email: dover@artimaging.com
Internet: http://www.dovertechsupport.com
The fastest way to receive technical support is via email or the Internet.

Design by Alan Weller and Juliana Trotta
Manufactured in the United States by Courier Corporation
48535801
www.doverpublications.com

RETRO KIDS
Patterns and Prints

What Baby Baby Boomers Wore

002

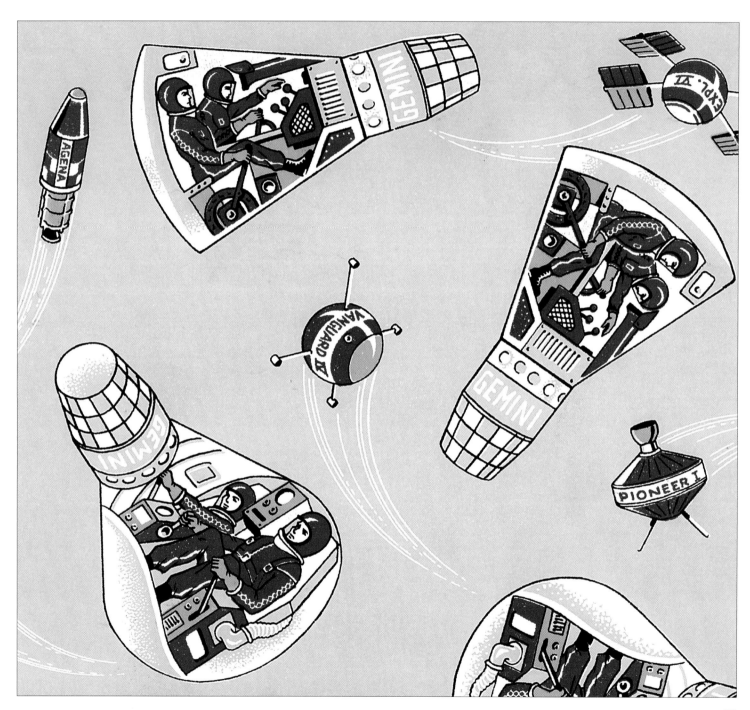

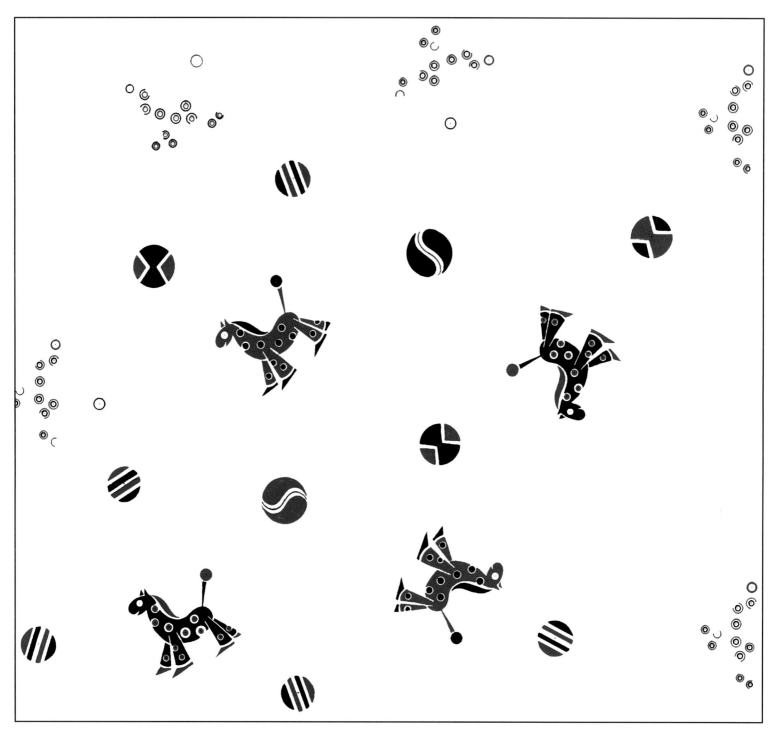

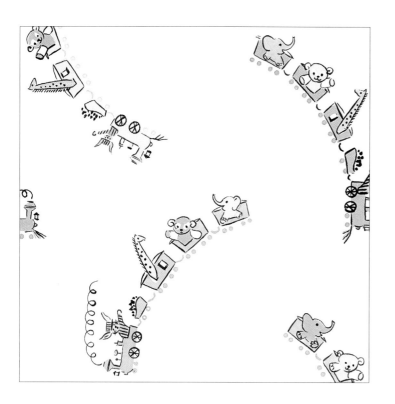

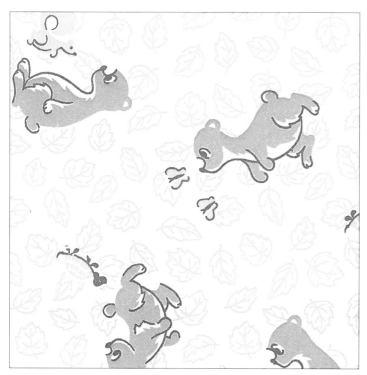

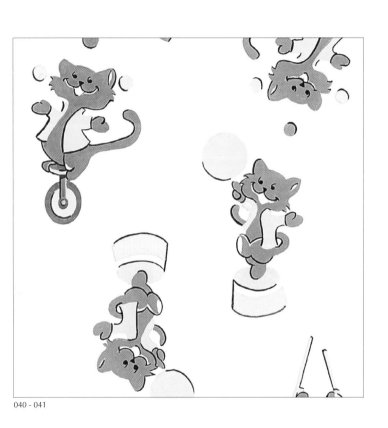

040 - 041

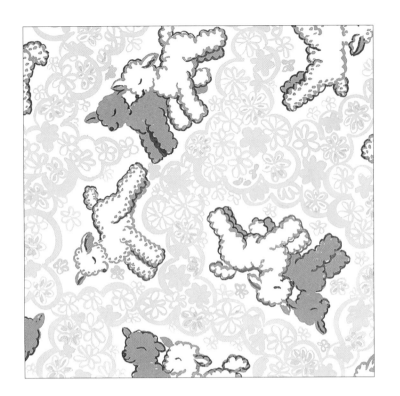
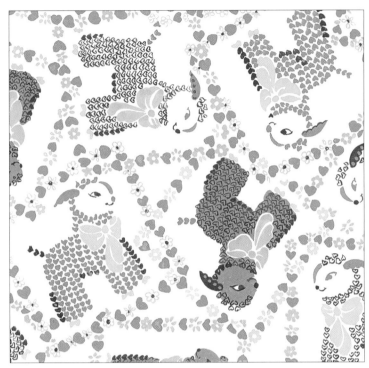
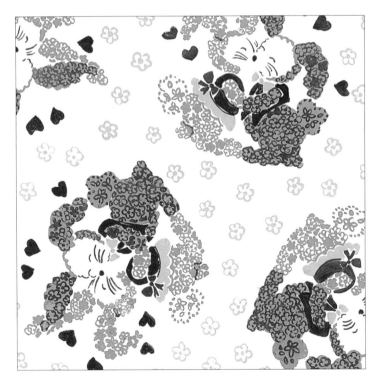

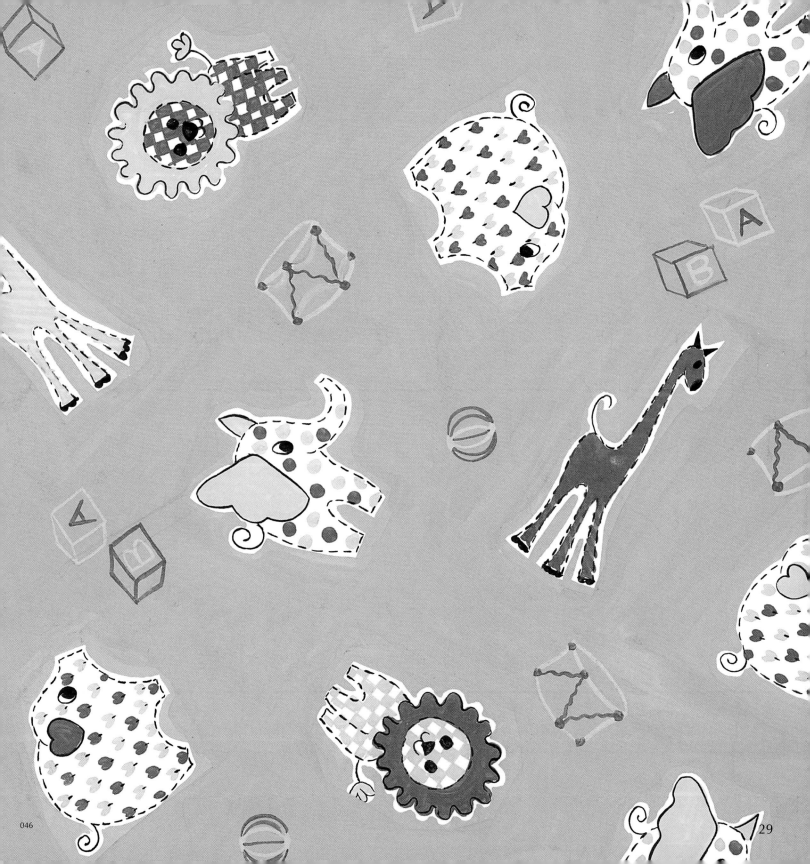

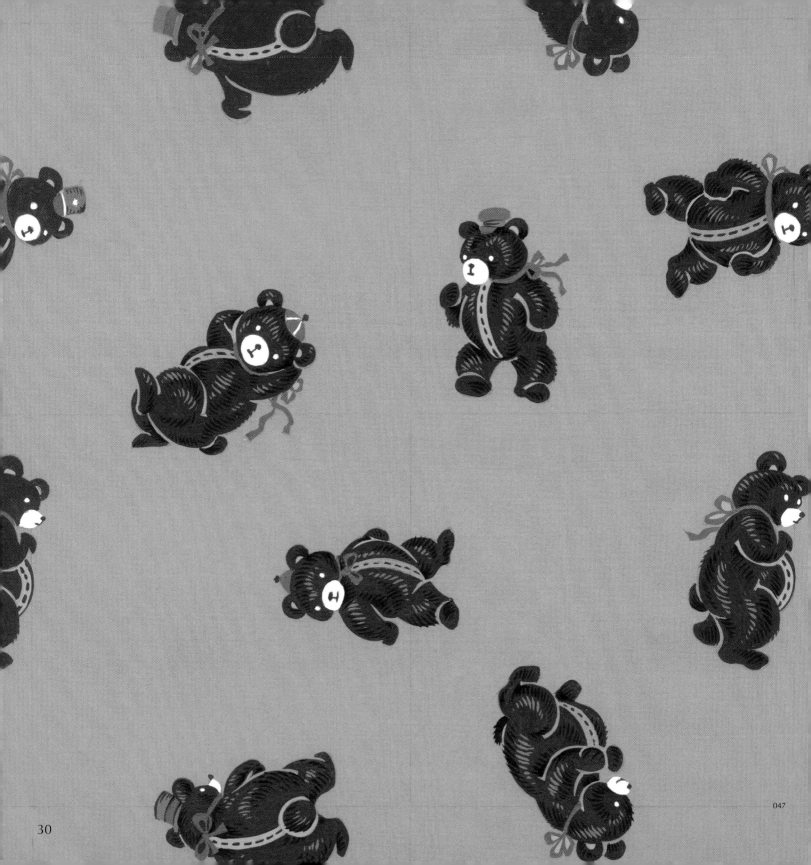

051

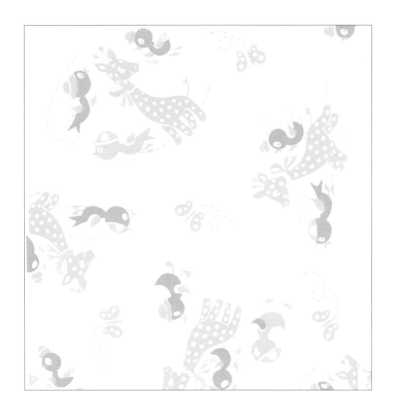

058 - 060

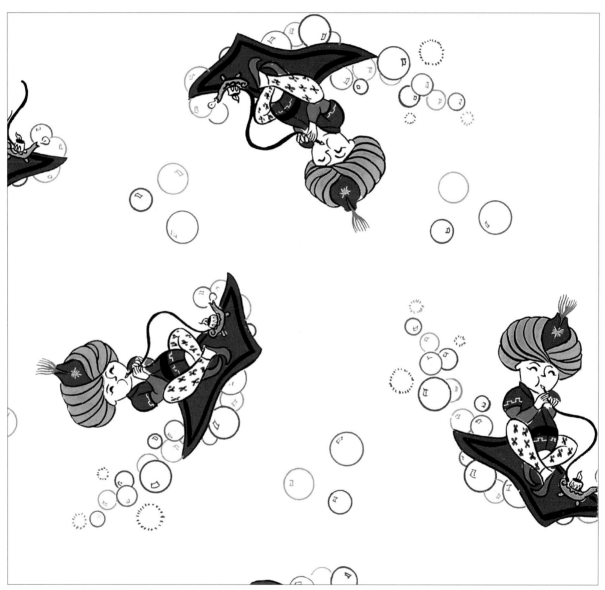

063

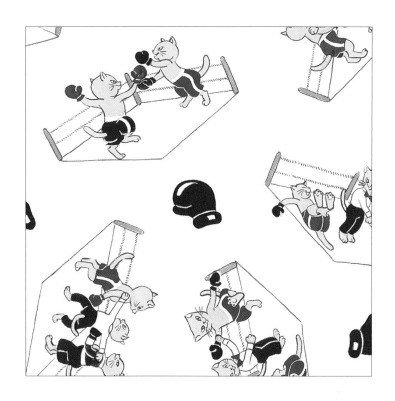

40

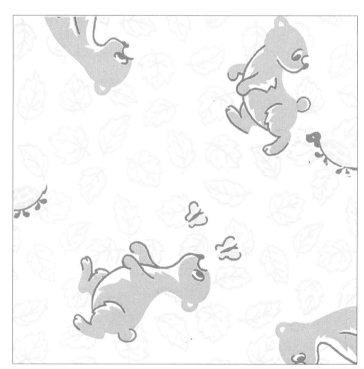

42

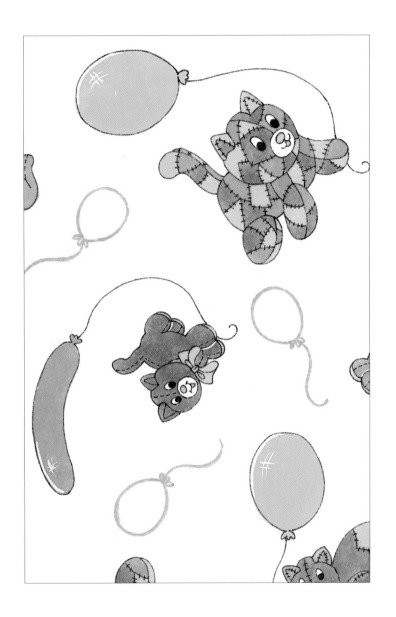

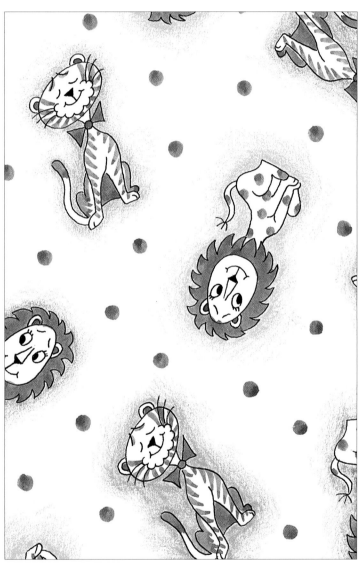

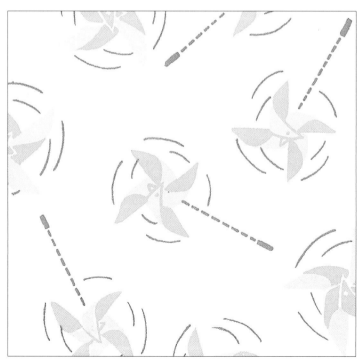

PAWS HERE

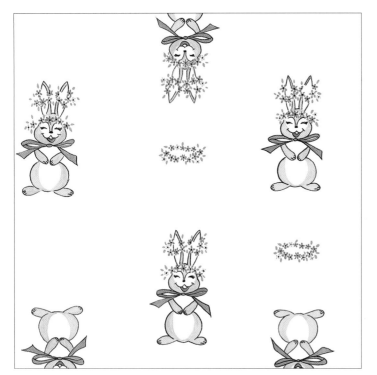

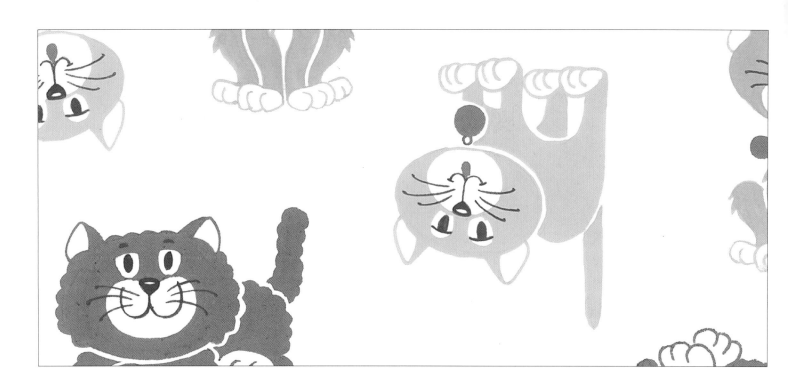

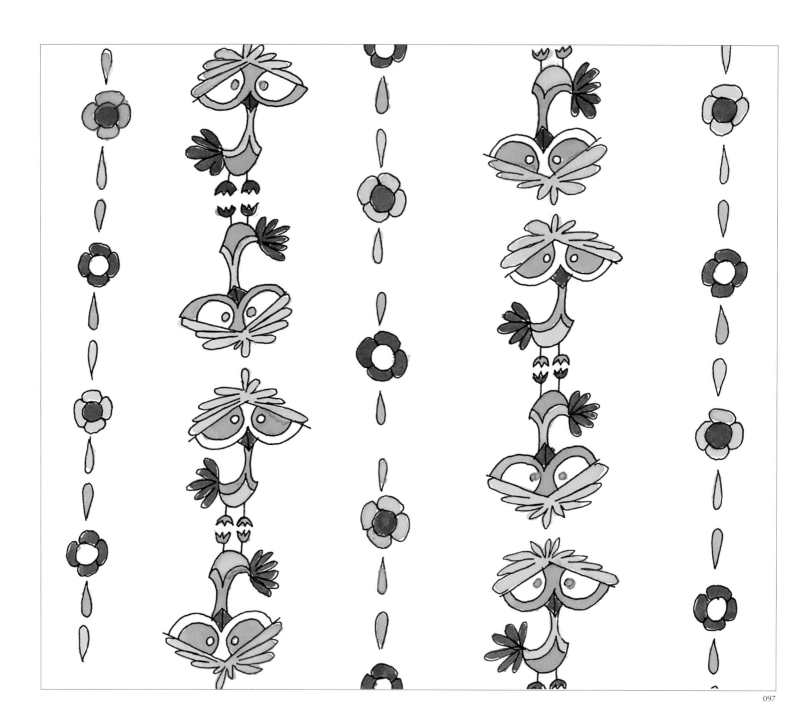

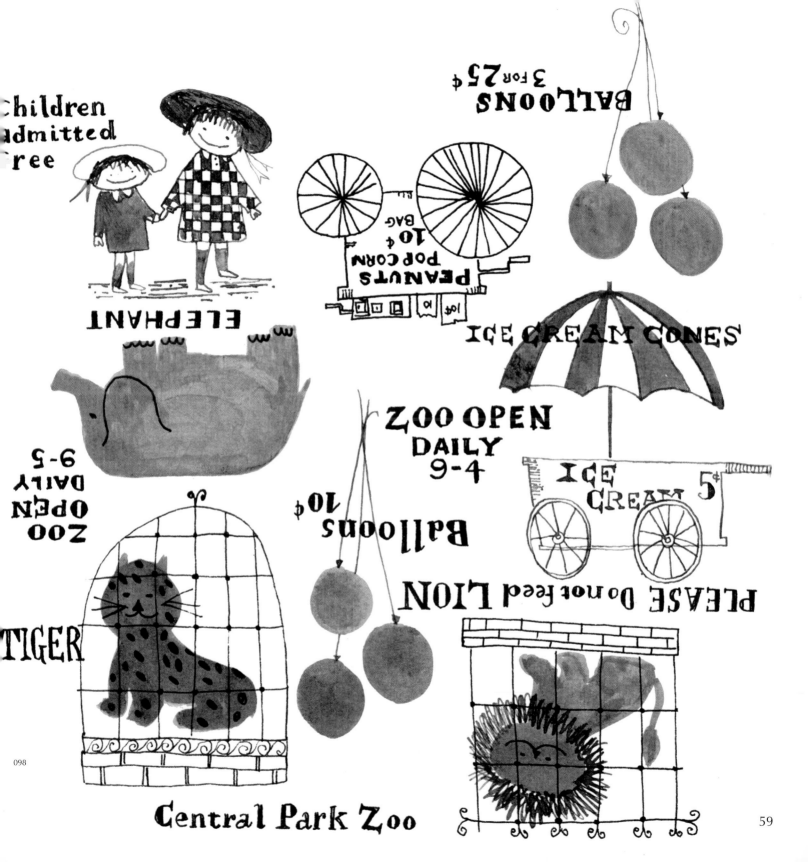

Central Park Zoo

099

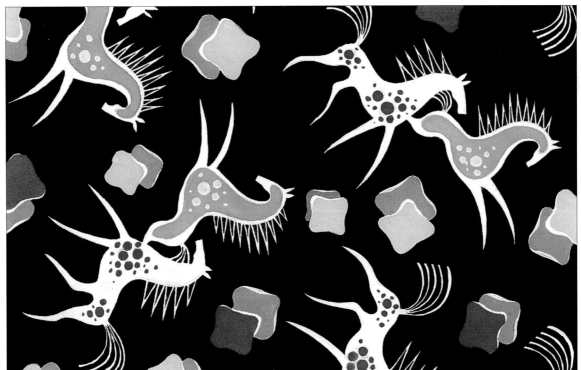

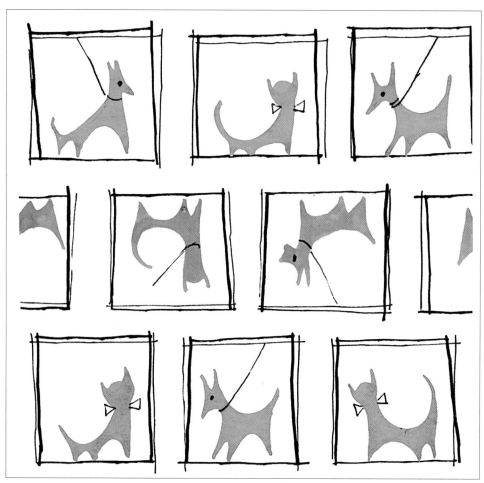

102

103

104

107

116

117

134

137

138 - 140

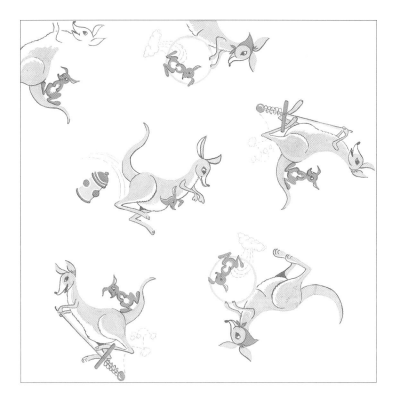

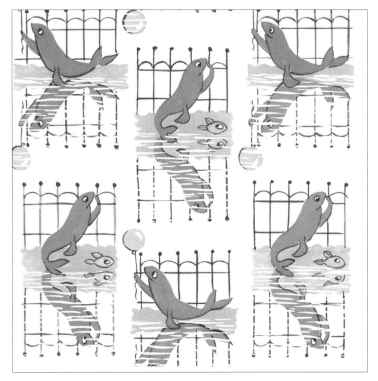

141 - 142

143

144 - 145

147

YOU MAKE ME HOP

153 - 154

155

157

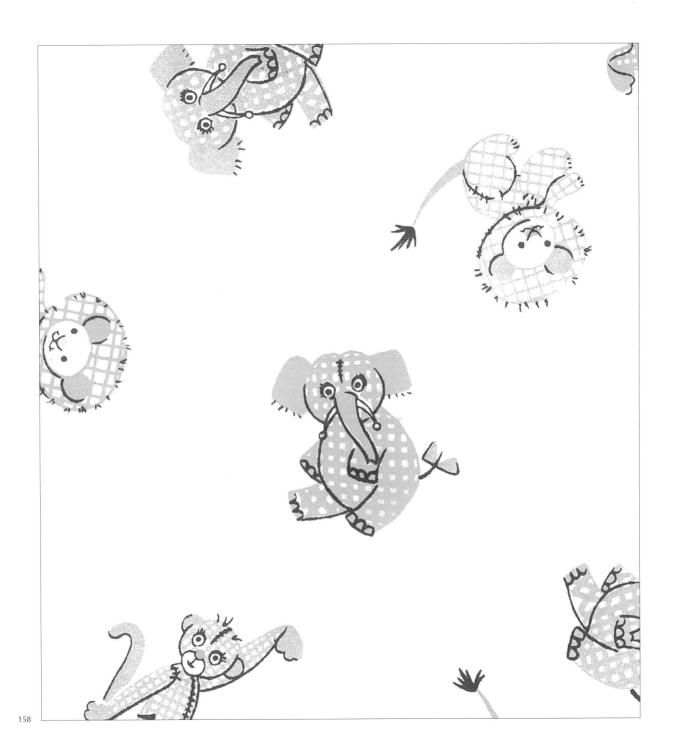

163

165 - 166

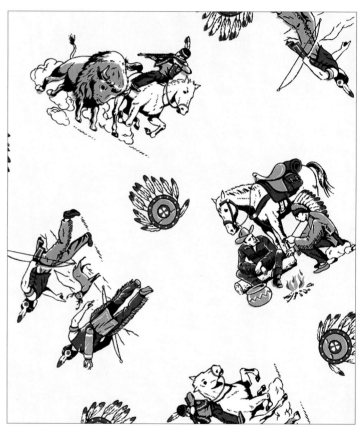

177 - 178

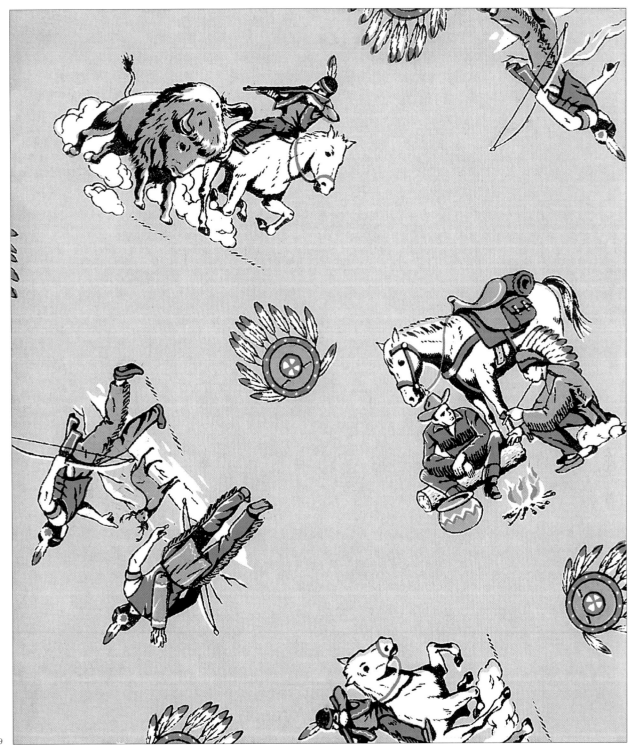

179

180

181 - 182

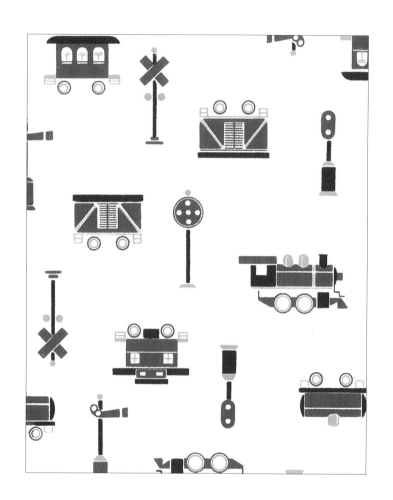
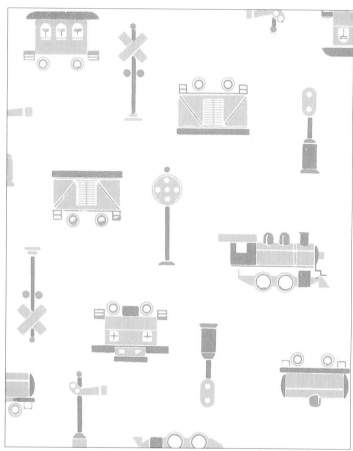

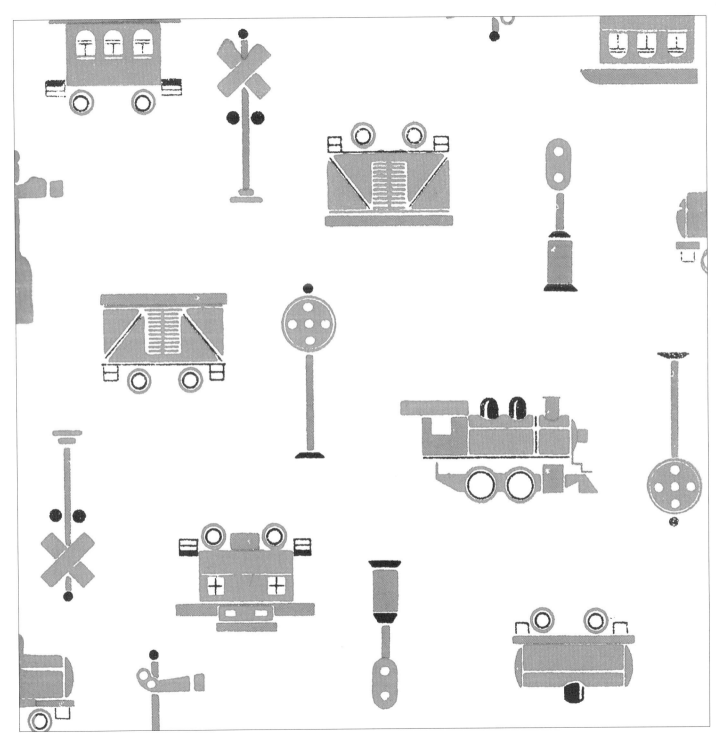

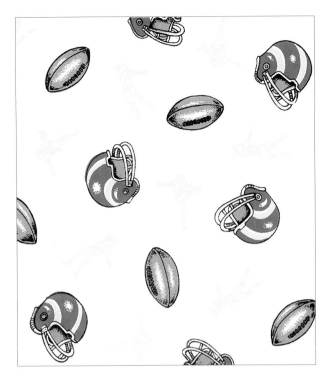
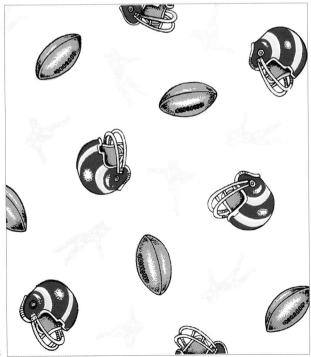

196

197 - 198

199 - 200

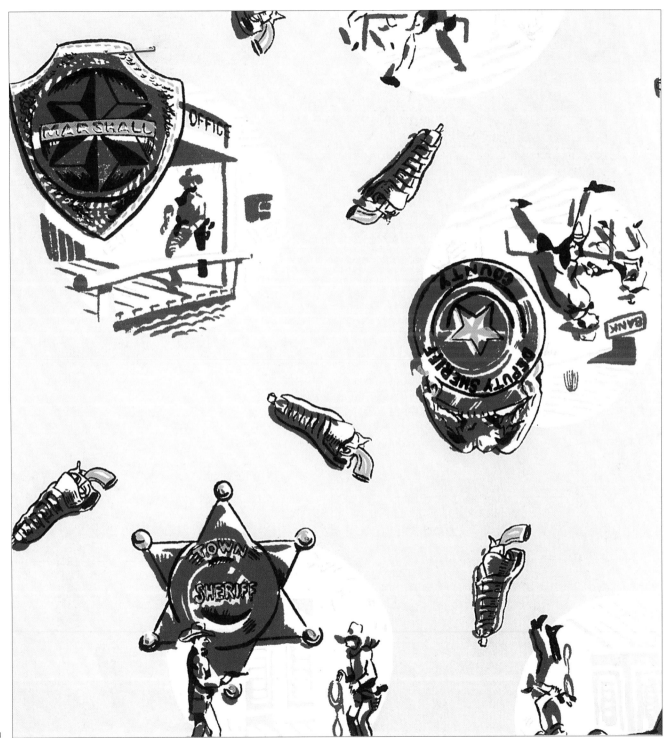

201

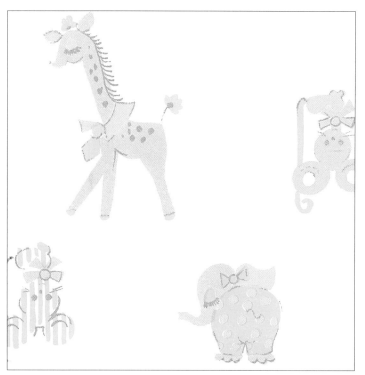

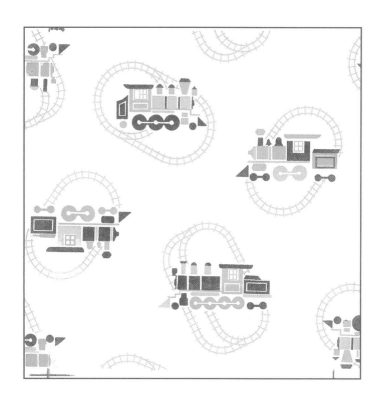

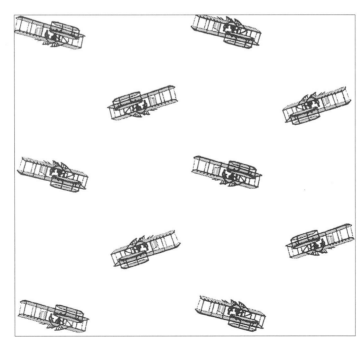

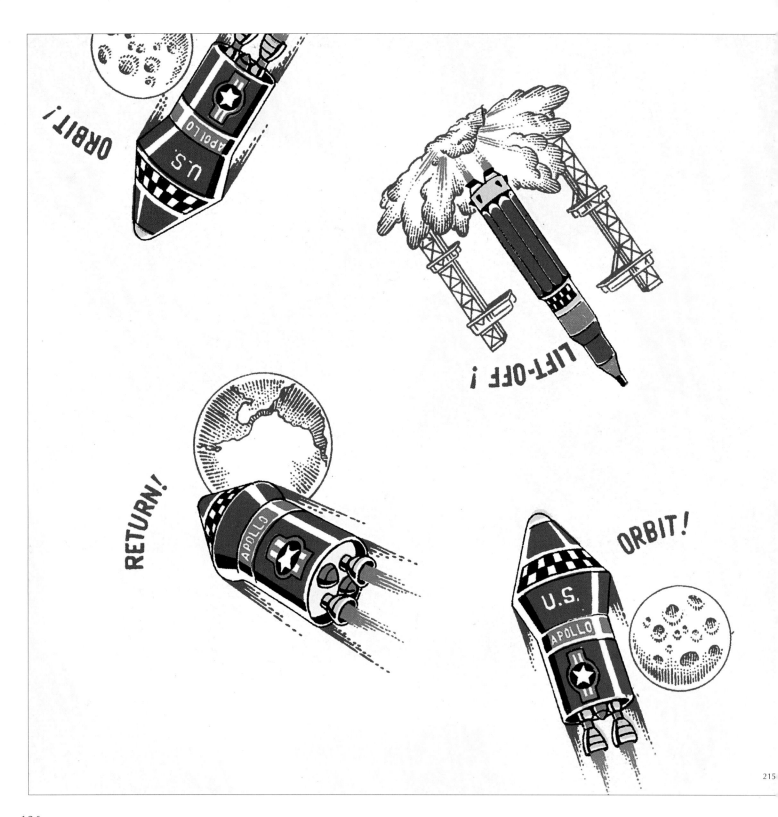

ORBIT!

LIFT-OFF!

RETURN!

ORBIT!

215

216